Spelling It Out

by Valerie Thomas

illustrated by Lew Keilar

Harcourt Achieve
Rigby • Saxon • Steck-Vaughn

www.HarcourtAchieve.com
1.800.531.5015

Characters

Sam

HB

The Principal

Contents

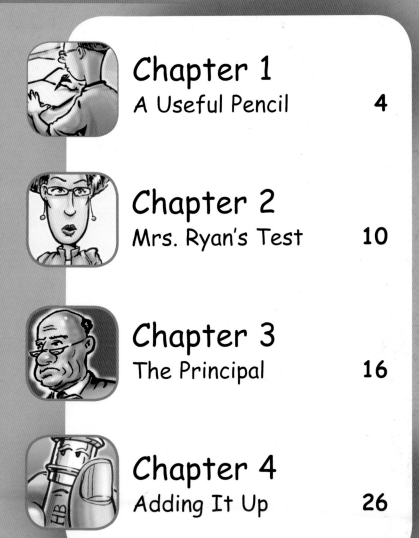

Chapter 1

A Useful Pencil

Sam was doing his homework.

"Friut is good for you," he wrote.

"Psst . . . hey you," said his pencil. "That is not how you spell *fruit.*"

Sam was surprised. He looked at the
pencil. It was a new HB pencil. There
was nothing on the pencil that said it
could talk.

"How do you spell it, then?" Sam asked.

"*F-r-u-i-t*," said the pencil.

Sam erased the *i* and the *u*, and wrote them in the right order.

"So are vegtables," he wrote.

"What!" shouted his pencil. "There's an
e after the g in *vegetables*."

Sam put in the e. Yes, that looked
much better.

The pencil was very rude, but it could spell. "This could be a very useful pencil," Sam thought.

Tomorrow was Friday.

Sam had a spelling test every Friday, so he decided to use the pencil. He'd never have to learn his spelling words again.

Chapter 2

Mrs. Ryan's Test

"Spelling test," said Mrs. Ryan.
"Vegetable," she said. "The first word is *vegetable*."

Sam knew that one now.

"*Pumpkin*," said Mrs. Ryan.

"That's a tricky word," thought Sam.

"Pumkin," he wrote.

"No! Don't you get it? There is a *p* after the *m*. It's *pumpkin*," the pencil shouted.

Everybody laughed. Sam turned bright red.

"Who said that?" asked Mrs. Ryan. She looked at Sam, but she knew it wasn't his voice.

"*Fruit,*" she said. Sam knew that word, too.

"*Raspberry*," she said.

"*R-a-s*," wrote Sam. He stopped.

"Keep going," shouted the pencil. "It's *p*, and then *berry*."

"Why is the *p* there?" asked Sam. "I don't hear any *p*."

13

Everybody laughed, but Mrs. Ryan was annoyed. "Was that you, Sam?" she asked.

"No, Mrs. Ryan," said Sam. "It was my pencil."

The whole class laughed even more.

"Don't be ridiculous," Mrs. Ryan said.
"Go see the principal."

Chapter 3

The Principal

Sam walked slowly to the principal's office. He was still holding the pencil.

"Why are you here?" the principal asked.

Sam didn't know what to say. "I couldn't spell *pumpkin* or *raspberry*."

"Well, you can practice them now," the princip' said.

"Pumkpin," Sam wrote, mixing up the second *p* and the *k*.

"Have you got a pumpkin for a brain?" shouted the pencil.

"No! Stop being such a bully," Sam said.

The principal looked at Sam.

"I was talking to my pencil, not you, sir." said Sam. "It shouts at me."

"I can fix that," said the principal. "Give me that pencil. You can use mine for now."

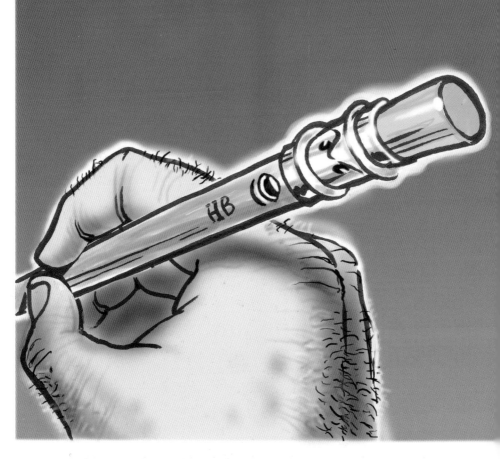

The principal started writing a letter. "Dear Parents," he wrote. "Next week all studants . . . "

"You silly man," shrieked the pencil. "Can't you spell *students*? How did you get to be principal?"

"Sam, did you say that?" the principal asked.

"No," said the pencil, "it's me, the pencil in your hand."

The principal looked at Sam and then at the pencil.

"I told you the pencil shouts," Sam said.

"Wow!" said the principal. "This could come in handy."

"But it's my pencil," said Sam.

"Actually," said the principal, "neither one of us should cheat with the pencil." Then the principal had an idea. "I think I should break this pencil."

"No!" shouted the pencil. Snap!

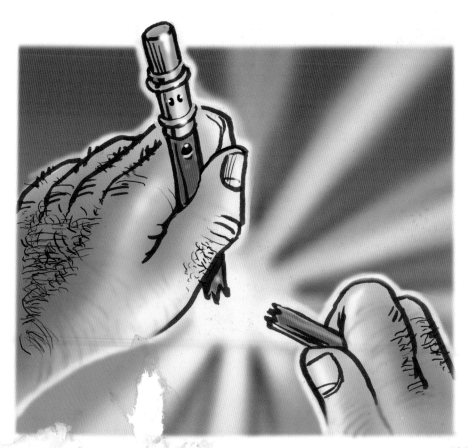

"Let's see if it still works," the principal
said.

" . . . all students will have a vacashun,"
the principal wrote.

"That's wrong," the pencil whispered.
"It's v . . . "

"Speak up," said Sam.

"I can't," sighed the pencil. "I'm only half the pencil I used to be."

Chapter 4

Adding It Up

That night Sam started his homework.
He wrote the heading *Elefants.*

"That's not right," whispered the pencil.
"You'd better look it up."

Sam picked up the dictionary. *Elephant*.
Sam had to look up 14 more words.
He knew the pencil couldn't help him
anymore. Then he realized that with
a little practice, he would become a
great speller!

Next came math. Sam decided to take out a new pencil. He started the first problem. 27 + 36 = 53

"No, no, no," screamed the pencil. "It's 63! Do I have to do *all* the work?"

"No way!" thought Sam, "I'm not going through this again. I like math, and at least I'm better at it than the principal."

Glossary

annoyed
slightly angry

dictionary
a book that gives the meanings of words

HB pencil
a hard, black pencil

homework
school work that is done at home

practice
to do something again and again until you improve

principal
the head of a school

shrieked
screamed in a high, loud voice

tricky
difficult

Valerie Thomas

What if someone invented a pencil like this? It could be like the spellcheck on a computer. The pencil could have a switch to turn off any shouting at school. Perhaps a light could flash when you make a mistake. What other ideas do you have?

Lew Keilar

All ♪ you Need is ♫ Love ♪

It turned out *all* Sam's pencils could sing and liked the Beatles most of all.